T0198514

WHAT WE CAN DO

Ariannis Hines

Illustrated by
Serafina Harris

To order additional copies of this book, contact:
Xlibris
844-714-8691
www.Xlibris.com
Orders@Xlibris.com

ISBN: Softcover   978-1-6641-3508-6
        EBook   978-1-6641-3507-9

Print information available on the last page

Rev. date: 10/02/2020

WHAT WE
CAN DO

What can we do? In time and space. What we do with our days affects our brains. Our brains are our biggest tool, and help to make us who we are.

We can create. Using our imaginations and uniting with the world around us, we will have creative and collaborative brains

We can watch a lot of TV. Turning off all signals beyond our eyes, we will have passive brains.

We can move. Running, dancing, playing, stretching, experimenting and moving our bodies, we will have active brains; expressive brains.

We can get enough sleep. Respecting when we need to recover from the business of the day, we will have refreshed and reliable brains.

We can be kind. Showing humility, compassion, saying, thinking, and doing nice things for others, laughing with others, being there for others when they need support, we will have happy brains.

We can remind ourselves that we were each created beautifully. Taking the time
to say kind things to ourselves, being patient with ourselves when we fail, we will have faithful and confident brains.

"I am enough"
"I am beautiful"
"I am an active listener"
"I speak my true thoughts with ease"
"I set clear boundaries"
"I am doing my best"

We can do dishonest things. With lying, cheating, and stealing, we will have confused brains.

Hi class!!
I was born in Canada.
But the birth
Certificate says
otherwise...

We can forgive. Forgiving others for the mean things they do, even if they do not say sorry, we will have understanding, empathetic brains.

We can live! What else can we do?

Printed in the United States
By Bookmasters